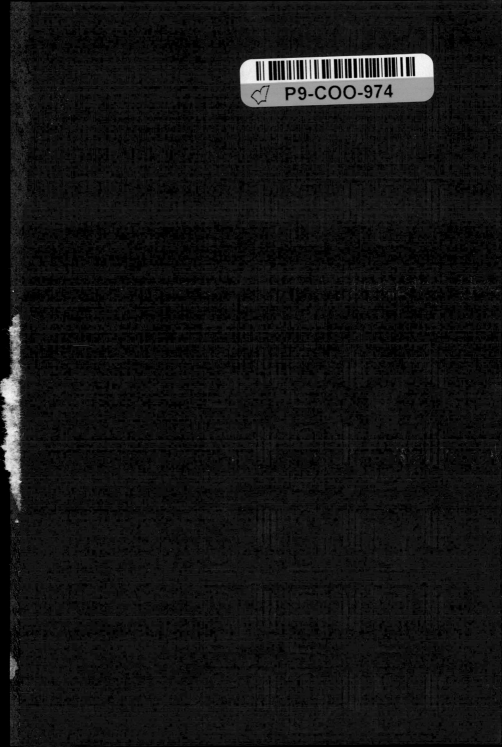

A TWENTY MINUTE SILENCE
FOLLOWED BY APPLAUSE

A TWENTY MINUTE SILENCE
FOLLOWED BY APPLAUSE

SHAWN WEN

Sarabande Books
Louisville, KY | Brooklyn, NY

Library of Congress Cataloging-in-Publication Data

Names: Wen, Shawn, author.
Title: A twenty minute silence followed by applause / Shawn Wen.
Description: First edition. | Louisville, KY : Sarabande Books, 2017.
Identifiers: LCCN 2016059115 | ISBN 9781941411483 (paperback)
Subjects: LCSH: Marceau, Marcel. | Mimes--France--Biography. | BISAC:
BIOGRAPHY & AUTOBIOGRAPHY / Literary. | PERFORMING ARTS /
Theater / Miming.
Classification: LCC PN1986.M3 W46 2017 | DDC 792.3/092--dc23
LC record available at https://lccn.loc.gov/2016059115

Interior and exterior design by Kristen Radtke.

Manufactured in Canada.
This book is printed on acid-free paper.
Sarabande Books is a nonprofit literary organization.

This project is supported in part by an award from the National Endowment for the Arts.
The Kentucky Arts Council, the state arts agency, supports Sarabande Books with state
tax dollars and federal funding from the National Endowment for the Arts.

For 问銀鸽 *and* 何惧

Also, always, of course: Chandler, Joe, Stephanie, and Talia

Why this black box? The bare stage? Why perform in a darkened, scraped-out spot?

The mime whirls his arms in the air. His gestures leave a trail: the awning, the veranda, the colonnade. A ghosted landscape rises up wherever his fingers point.

Before there was a thing, there was nothing. Earth was formless and empty. Such was the base. God created the world in dark space. The matter that we touch, see, and feel—the architecture and the moss—those were the remnants.

No matter how hard we try, things that exist will never outnumber things that do not exist.

YOUNG MARCEAU

September 1939, Germany invaded Poland. Then France entered the war and the people of Strasbourg were told they had two hours to pack sixty pounds of belongings each. Marcel was sixteen. He and his brother Alain were among the first to flee.

His brother emerged as a leader of the Underground in Limoges. Marcel became a forger. With red crayons and black ink, he shaved years off the lives of French children, too young now to be sent to concentration camps. He dressed them up as boy scouts and campers and held their hands as they went high into the Alps. Over the mountain and through the woods, out of occupied France and into Switzerland.

His brother's name appeared on a wanted list tacked to the wall of Gestapo headquarters.

Marcel Mangel left Limoges for Paris and changed his name.

he imitated everything though
it wasn't imitation
it was play, wasn't play
he was a bird, the shape
of plants and trees
spoke silence, the language of fish
the body is boneless, loose
like elastic, the form
of anything that vibrates or throbs

MANGEL

His father was a Jew, a butcher, a communist.
The name was Mangel, meaning "lack" or "deficiency."
His father went to Auschwitz, the body
taken to the crematorium
before his identity was recorded in the log.

+++

Marcel Marceau preferred not to reveal his given name. He thought that "Mangel" was too common in France. Too many people came forward claiming to be relations.

He borrowed "Marceau" from a general in Napoléon's army.

"Everyone in the Underground changed his name. You had to in order to survive."

PEDAGOGY

After the war, Marceau joined Charles Dullin's School of Dramatic Art, in Paris, intent on becoming an actor.

"We were alone on stage, making funny movements and not speaking."

Teachers at Dullin's school had a dream. They wanted to create a new poetics of theater to supplant the decadence and mediocrity. In early twentieth-century Paris, stage actors focused entirely on their voices and facial expressions. Their bodies were inexpressive anchors. Then, a writer named Jacques Copeau, who at thirty-three had never set foot on a stage, envisioned a renewal: Actors who were also playwrights. Actors who performed without words on a bare stage. The body was their text.

Étienne Decroux: intellectual, theoretician, teacher, actor. As a young anarchist, he enrolled in performing arts school to study political oratory. But his path was diverted, and soon he brought all his dogmatism and verbosity to mime. Decroux sneered at bumbling pantomimes who flailed about onstage. "That play of face and hands which seemed to try to explain things but lacked the needed words. I detested this form." His wordless theater stepped over hapless romantics and their flower-seller girlfriends. Decroux wanted to train and isolate the body. To shift gravity, challenge balance, create a physics of compensation. He called this *corporeal mime*. "Art should be serious after all."

Leave speech behind. The body has its own language: weight, resistance, hesitation, surprise. Decroux was so obsessed with the purity of his new art that for years he taught and performed completely nude. He took to wearing loincloths only when he realized that his audience was distracted. Marceau later said of his teacher, "The work was very beautiful, but abstract, not unlike the Cubists."

Decroux met Marceau, taught Marceau, and proclaimed the young actor a natural mime.

The critic Walter Kerr later wrote of Decroux, "It is the teacher's fate never to be incomparable himself; he frees talent to go where he cannot go."

Of course, Marceau was not a Cubist. His work was far from abstract. He created the beloved Bip. He kissed the hand of Charlie Chaplin for birthing the Little Tramp. He thanked Charles Dickens for his Pip. But when historians and critics whispered *Pierrot, Pierrot,* Marceau responded, "Pierrot was a French figure; Bip is a citizen of the world."

BIP IS BORN

It's 1947. Two years after the war, we meet the fool.

"My eyebrows are too close together, which can give a hard look to the face. To seem more naïve, I drew false eyebrows very high, about two or three centimeters above . . ."

Bip in the subway
Bip the street musician
Bip as a china salesman
Bip takes an ocean voyage
Bip as a lion tamer
Bip hunts butterflies
Bip as the botany professor
Bip at the dance hall
Bip as the tailor in love
Bip makes dynamite
Bip the big game hunter
Bip goes to an audition
Bip at the restaurant
Bip dreams he is Don Juan
Bip as a babysitter
Bip looks for a job on New Year's Eve
Bip goes to the moon
Bip and the bumblebee
Bip as a fireman
Bip has a sore finger

SCENE 1: BIP, THE SOLDIER

The first helmet is too small, resting squarely on top of his head. The second helmet is much too big, and it falls over his face. The last one balances perfectly. He ties it underneath his chin, then struggles to fit himself into a tiny waistcoat. He misaligns the buttons of a long jacket and painstakingly refastens them. Bip preparing for basic training is identical to Bip primping for a gala. The same movements, the same romantic music. A new surrounding narrative.

Bip takes a large gulp of water from his canteen. Missiles soar overhead. He shares water with a soldier to his left. The explosions get louder. He ducks down and covers his head. After this round of bombing stops, he tries to put his arm around the comrade for comfort, but he grasps only air. As he feels for his friend, his hand lowers to the ground, finally resting just a few inches above the stage floor, as if touching the back of a corpse. He pulls the soldier up on his lap and rests his head against the man's chest, listening for a heartbeat.

GENEALOGY

Before there was Bip, there was Pedrolino, a stock character in the commedia dell'arte, the youngest son of the Italian performance family. He who slept in the straw with animals, sharing the dogs' half-starved lives.

Molière painted Pedrolino white and taught him French. He was reborn as Pierrot. Jean-Gaspard Deburau turned Pierrot into a mute.

Jean-Louis Barrault resurrected Pierrot in Marcel Carné's film classic, *Les Enfants du Paradis*, the movie referred to as France's answer to *Gone with the Wind*.

Four men vie for the love of a beautiful courtesan Garance, the movie's proxy for commedia's Columbina. But the man whose love is purest, the man who suffers most in pursuit, is the whitefaced mime. A Pierrot, a Pierrot, here named "Baptiste Deburau."

Barrault himself appeared in *Les Enfants du Paradis*. He was the sad-faced clown dressed in white. The trusting fool, butt of pranks. Naïve, moonstruck dreamer. Ultimately, Columbina broke his heart and ran away with Harlequin, friend and rival and, later, Marceau's first role in a play called *Baptiste*.

When journalists asked about Bip, *the trusting fool, butt of pranks*, Marceau dismissed Bip's European ancestors. He credited the American silent film stars: Chaplin, Keaton, Laurel and Hardy.

At least one person saw through it. Theater critic Edward Thorpe wrote in *The London Evening Standard*, "I must confess to never having liked Bip anyway. Despite the debt to Chaplin, the character is close to Pierrot and the winsome whimsical commedia dell'arte crew, with his affected walks, limp-wristed manner, silly hats and bizarre costumes that look like a cross between little Lord Fauntleroy and an eighteenth-century sailor."

(A nod to those who came before him? Marceau named his first child, a son, Baptiste.)

SCENE 2: BIP, GREAT STAR OF THE TRAVELING CIRCUS

Knife throwing is a feat of precision. How can we gauge our virtuoso's aim when both the woman and the knives are invisible? Marceau trains our ears. He taps the stage floor with his ballet flat, creating an audible thud for each knife that successfully misses the woman and hits the board. We start with a symphony of thuds, a quick series of successful throws. He's an expert. But his mood darkens as the challenges mount. He turns around and holds out one hand like a compact mirror, tossing the knife over his shoulder. Again, we hear the reassuring whump of a knife on the board.

Chin high, unmistakable look of pride on his face. He ties a blindfold around his eyes and pulls out a sword half the size of his body. He throws it with a heave. Silence. Still blindfolded, he waves to the crowd and takes a bow. He yanks out the sword and, finally, sound of her body hitting the ground. No matter. He exits stage left.

M. ON SPEECH

"I don't suffer from silence. I could be two days without speaking. I wouldn't suffer at all."

Marcel Marceau's first wife divorced him in 1958. She said he would not speak to her for days on end. She called it mental cruelty. He called it rehearsal.

His third wife Anne Sicco called mime "his only way of thinking and expressing himself."

But then Studs Terkel said, "Only one guy outtalked me. Marcel Marceau. I couldn't get a word in."

He used his hands as he spoke.

There used to be a rumor that he was a deaf mute. He dispelled this rumor by appearing on talk shows: Johnny Carson, Flip Wilson, Merv Griffin.

"I'm obliged to talk. I don't like to talk especially."

But Marcel Marceau had a reputation. Those who conversed with him found his conversation as entertaining as his stage performance. His English was nearly flawless.

"I think I am not so different from other people in my private life. Except that I don't like very much to socialize. I am rather a person who is on his own, I like to paint, I like to read, to write, and I travel so much, you know?"

There's a joke that Marcel Marceau released an album. The record consists of twenty minutes of silence followed by applause.

M. ON MARCEAU

Marceau liked to recite lines from his own reviews: "'Marceau explains why theater exists, where it comes from, and why it will be with us for a long time.'"

But that's not what the critic said.

Walter Kerr actually wrote, "Marceau really explains where the theater came from, why it is going to last for a very long time, and why we like it."

21

Kerr did not write "Marceau explains why theater exists." That was Marceau on Marceau.

The empty stage is a universe without laws. Up to the mime to conjure and rearrange, to make the dark space become alive with recognitions and quickenings. To him, absences can be transformed into a wall, a woman, a restaurant, a thief. The mime holds out his arms and motions that the world floats within the armspan of one man.

SCENE 3: BIP AT A SOCIETY PARTY

He fastens a bow tie around his neck. First one arm through the jacket, then the other. When he pulls on gloves, his fingers wriggle into place like burrowing animals. His movements are slow, familiar, and precise.

At the coat check, there's a struggle to peel off his gloves. Then his coat sleeves cling to his arms. He bends backwards and rips himself out of the jacket. He puts up his fists, ready to box.

Friends from across the room catch his eye and he gives them a warm wave, *Hello*. He lingers with the last girl, raising his eyebrow suggestively, then moves through the room, schmoozing. A giant and a dwarf are in line to greet him, prompting Bip to point his gaze toward the ceiling, then the floor. Double take: Are they a couple?

Bip commences a handshaking tour, but exhaustion creeps into his eyes. One man won't let go of his right hand, another grabs his left hand, locking him into a straitjacketed greeting.

Bip pours himself a drink and downs it. The pork chop on his plate behaves like a rubber ball. He saws at it back and forth, but the knife slips, shooting the meat to the floor. When no one's watching he surreptitiously slides down in his chair, grabs it, and again cleaves away. Finally takes a bite, and plainly finds the food disgusting, though he struggles to keep a dignified expression on his face. Finally, he washes the mess down with water, stands, throws his hands out and spins.

Spinning is part of Marceau's visual language. It's shorthand for a change in character, a switch in location, the end of a performance. While Bip twirls with one hand over his mouth to hold down vomit, Marceau is marking a new scene.

Dinner's over. Bip has recovered, accepts a cigarette. He delightedly blows smoke rings in the air and pokes his finger through them. Rests his elbow on a mantel and appears to be chatting with good friends, relaxed for the first time this evening. He accepts another drink, one more. We read his steady intoxication in arm flops, shoulders heavier with each glass, and when he gets up to leave, he's stumbling drunk. He hangs on to invisible walls for balance. Grasps at the arms of fellow partygoers for support. Again a wrestling match with the jacket and the gloves. At last, he's out the door, throws his head back and spins.

COLLECTIONS: WORK-RELATED READING

Philological Entertainment.
(David-Étienne Choffin)

Dramatic Anecdotes.
(Jean Marie Bernard Clément and Joseph de La Porte)

Old Paris: Parties, Games and Shows.
(Victor Fournel)

Memoirs of Goldoni, Written by Himself: Forming a Complete History of His Life and Writings.
(Carlo Goldoni)

Lyon's Guignol Theater Illustrated.
(Jean-Baptiste Onofrio and Eugène Lefebvre)

Acrobats and Mountebanks.
(Hugues Le Roux and Jules Garnier)

Pulcinella: Former King of Puppets Becomes a Philosopher.
(Alcide-Joseph Lorentz)

Memories of the Funambulists.
(Champfleury)

The Two Pierrots.
(Champfleury)

Masks and Jesters [Italian Comedy].
(Maurice Sand)

Lyric Theatre.
(Venard de La Jonchère)

Grotesque Paris: The Celebrities of the Street.
(Charles Yriarte)

From the Sword to the Stage.
(Robert Heddle-Roboth and Daniel Marciano)

M. ON AMERICA, 1955

He arrives in New York for a two-week run. But
the Americans hold him over, and he stays for six
months. Originally slated to perform at the Phoe-
nix Theater, he moves on to the Ethel Barrymore
on Broadway. From there, City Center. Applause
begins before he even steps onstage.

A figure in the deep
White
Because it shows movement
White
Because it hides the wrinkles
White
Because we are frail

Marceau said, "Americans love something new. And
I was doing something new. I brought silence on
stage for the first time. I made the invisible visible, I
created metaphors, and Americans saw the poetry."

As Chaplin danced and bumbled, Marceau studied
the footwork.

"I found the art in that silence."

And he sold it.

SCENE 4: BIP PLAYS DAVID AND GOLIATH

Stage right, Bip hunches over to make himself slight, all rollicking feet and fluttering digits.

Stage left, hulking Goliath, arms raised on either side, face grim, muscles bouncing with each step.

David weakly pantomimes boxing. He clasps his hands together into a prayer and glances at the sky. Goliath approaches in stilted, bold steps, arms waving like a gorilla's.

David peers into the audience, pleading for help. Fear has compressed his body.

Goliath bounds across the stage with an enormous jumping jack, searching for his prey. He clenches and unclenches his fists.

In a single, swift movement, David launches a rock with his slingshot. Goliath stumbles back, wide-eyed, and darkness overcomes him.

M. ON THE CONNECTIVE TISSUES

Collagen fibers
Braided, banded, packed
Coalesce
Into macroaggregates, into fascicles and tendons
These little bundles of string tie muscle to bone
They stretch and spring
tear, inflame

"I don't mime to look nice or cute. It must be
tense."

Ligaments are elastic
Under tension, they lengthen
The body stretches
Supple joints flower

"Do you make them laugh under the belt, or do
you make them laugh with an idea? The best is
laughter through tears, a laugh that hurts."

Cutaneous
Of the skin
The nerve endings react
To heat and cold
To touch

"The more I play now, the better I feel in my muscles, in my control."

I am the pant legs
I am the pant legs
I flare
I never hug the ankles
I bloom out

M. ON HIS OWN

"I had the feeling there was no war going on, so kind were the people and so warm the welcome." (May 1970, Hanoi)

He claims that he cannot tell his fans apart. French, American, Vietnamese—all citizens defined by their adoration for him. He says they laugh and cry at the same moments. With a flick of his fingers, he reaches in and pulls out identical sighs. He takes in the onlookers, the gigglers and gaspers, the criers—all from behind the shadow of a hand.

His hand, with all its particulars. Each line, bulge, and groove—defined. They tell the story of a man.

The fingerprints are proof.

He wanted the universal, commonality across nations. But what if all people were not alike? From France to America to Vietnam. He found no formula for the end of suffering. No formula to stir up empathy and understanding. Just a formula for one man.

SCENE 5: BIP ATTEMPTS SUICIDE

The girl in the framed photo doesn't return his feelings, so he's looking for a way out. He places his battered hat on the floor, safely out of the splash zone. Bip weighs the options: poison, pistol, dagger, gas, and noose.

He mixes the poison himself, and the elixir is so appetizing. Sweet nectar's all drunk up and he feels fine.

32   So, Bip goes for the pistol. He covers his ear with his free hand. Such delicate sensibilities. The gun shakes uncontrollably in his nervous grip.

His aim is too high, then too low. He tightens his grasp. But, wait, where is the heart? To the left or right of the sternum? He feels along his chest with the barrel, trying to recall science class. By accident the gun goes off and the sound terrifies him. Stunned, trembling, he reconsiders.

Director: Marcel, it's beautiful.
Marceau: I made two or three mistakes but fortunately you didn't see them.

M. ON BOUNDARIES AND BORDERLINES

"Mime can't translate lies. For lies, words are adequate."

"I could use words, but to be very honest, it's beautiful to be a mime. Words would destroy the mystery of the illusion."

"Mime can do things that words cannot. . . . It describes the metaphysical world on the border of the real world."

He made you do it.

SCENE 6: BIP, THE BULLFIGHTER

He's the matador crowned with an iconic three-pointed hat, his stovetop perched on the fence beside the bullring.

He dances. He's a parading spider. The sweep of his arms conjures up a full stadium and its crowd. He allows his cape to catch in the air and billow. Before the fight starts, he takes a moment to lean on a shelf and take a breath. (A charming disruption of the narrative, and typical Bip, the furniture materializes and dematerializes at will.)

From a distance, the bull stares him down. Bip is not up to the task. He daintily dangles the cape away from his body, terrified of the bull drawing near.

Long pause. The bull refuses to charge.

Bip points to the cape. He drags the bull like a disobedient dog on a leash. He leans on the mantel again to catch his breath.

Drumroll begins. He rotates, making sure the arena crowd sees his weapon. In a swift motion, he spears the bull. There's a flicker of regret on his face; then he assumes a triumphant pose, arms up and chest inflated. He tips his cap towards the audience and they burst into applause.

Were you horrified? Did you think he wouldn't go through with it? Bip breaks out of his exultant stance to revive the bull. He bends over to pet it, grabs the udders and begins to squeeze. The bull transforms into a docile heifer. Bip sticks his finger into the milk to give it a taste.

M. ON MAN'S MODERN PROBLEMS

Coming off his US tour, and just a day before heading off to the USSR, Marceau stops in at the studios of Guy Béart's new show *Bienvenue*. The taping has the feel of a master class. Photogenic audience members crowd the stage, seated right next to the host. The camera turns to them frequently as they applaud, chuckle, and ask questions. They look like idealized graduate students: beautiful, curious, and young.

Marceau is dressed in a black suit that's tailored perfectly to his lean body. He's thirty-three years old and the most handsome he's ever looked. Béart reminds his audience the mime has arrived "without the white mask, without the character he immortalized—Bip—without the hat, without the flower." This sets the tone for today's intimate show.

Marceau steps on stage and begins: "The mime must be clear with his gestures. A mime who we cannot understand is a solipsistic man," he says, prompting quiet laughter.

Marceau takes off his suit jacket and hands it to a guy sitting close by. He opens with *The Kite*. The strength of the wind appears to lift him, bending his whole body backwards. He fights against the gust of air, forcing himself to the ground. This is Decroux's *contrepoids* in action. A few audience members scream, exhilarated by the palpable illusion of wind, as Marceau shifts his weight from one foot to the other, hot under the closeup adoration.

He pretends to wait for an elevator, "one of man's modern problems." Marceau anxiously looks up at the indicator lights, presses the button multiple times and then gives up, taking the stairs. To the audience's delight, he punctuates the long climb by marching impatiently around the landing at each floor.

The routine employs another Decroux technique: *raccourci*, or "shortcut"—a more abstract trick. The actor distills a movement into its basic elements while keeping the action recognizable. The stylized gesture compresses space and time as the mime climbs stairs, walks through the Garden of Eden, or skates across the rink, remaining in place. Hours seem to pass in seconds, years in minutes.

A young woman raises her hand, "How do I become the greatest mime in the world?"

"A very difficult question to answer," Marceau says. "There are great mimes, for example Harpo Marx." An excuse to break into a series of impressions: Buster Keaton, Stan Laurel, Charlie Chaplin. The audience hoots at Marceau's figures from their childhood.

"When you are abroad, if you do not understand the language, do you talk with your hands? And is that mime?" asks another young woman.

Marceau pulls out a caricature of an Italian man, pinching his fingers to his thumb, mumbling under his breath, pulling his lower eyelid down with his index finger, *Beware, I'm watching you.*

"We eat an apple," he says, holding up an invisible sphere, demonstrating its shape and weight. "Volume." He takes a bite. The crunch of the fruit gives way to pulp. Juice spills out of his full mouth. He inhales deeply, savoring the taste, and then tosses the core to the ground. "Orange," he announces, unpeeling the thick rind, separating the individual carpels, and biting into the flesh. "Ice cream." He takes a spoonful, and his smiling eyes are shocked with pain, teeth chattering from brain freeze.

Beads of sweat drip down his cheek, glistening at his hairline. A woman starts to ask a question,

"Monsieur Marceau, I want to know . . . ," but he cuts her off.

"Animals are extraordinary mimes," he says. Marceau imitates the wide, dilated pupils of his own pet, a Siamese kitten. "And the tail! He scares himself. He turns around." Marceau arches his back in a cat's defensive stance and takes three lateral jumps.

Another woman raises her hand. "Tell me, in pantomime, I love you."

"Ah, I did not expect this question," Marceau says. "It's so French."

Marceau mimes the nineteenth-century Pierrot, lovelorn, clutching his heart, kissing the air, one arm extended towards his beloved.

Or: Marceau leans against a shelf and leers at a woman across the room. He flicks cigarette ash on the ground, saunters over, and grabs her.

Or: He walks up to the female audience member, pulls her out of her chair, and kisses her on both cheeks.

M. ON CHAPLIN

Marceau said, "How far back can I summon memories of the past? When I was five years old, my mother took me to see Charlie Chaplin's silent moving pictures. Ah, Chaplin! To us he was a god. He made us laugh and cry, purged us of our own misfortunes, showed us a thousand tricks. And, always, no matter how beaten down, he triumphed over his tribulations in the end."

The first mime company did not rehearse. They were children on parade. Children flying banners fashioned from tattered handkerchiefs. Children wielding tree branches as rifles and canes. Waterloo in front of them. Narrow streets behind them. A dozen little Little Tramps battling the police.

Marceau's show returns in fragments. Your mind has been trained by the still camera. You can capture an instant, a flash; the mime inhabits a dozen positions. But your imagination cannot complete a sequence. Videos and photographs remind you how transient the stage is. So you replay the dancing ghost in your head and pray to get it right.

SCENE 7: BIP AS SKATER AND SPECTATOR

The white floor suggests a sheet of ice. Bip enters stage left, placing one foot in front of the other in a deliberately flat-footed walk. Taking a moment to admire the other skaters, he leans on an imaginary guideline, his torso slightly bouncing against its natural tension.

Upstage, there are two pillars. He rests his hat on one and pulls himself up on the other, so that his feet dangle over the floor. He laces his skates and waxes the blades. In a show of extra preparation, he applies wax to his armpits and chest, and then warms up with a few stretches.

Bip's gaze populates the empty stage with a crowd of holiday revelers. As he follows a particularly skilled skater, his upper body rocks aspirationally from side to side. His head weaves in a figure eight as she glides around the rink. But his interest turns to derision. She takes a spill on the ice. He laughs and points at her. The mishap gives him a bout of courage and he lowers himself onto the ice.

His ankles give way and legs collapse. Embarrassed, Bip climbs back on one pillar and pretends he's happy to be a spectator.

On his final attempt, he starts off timidly, ankles bent inward. His body begins to wobble and he throws his arms out for balance. He swims the breaststroke, then freestyle, trying to catch an air current strong enough to allow him to stay upright. Finally, he shifts his weight from one leg to the other, skating briskly towards the audience. Beaming with happiness, he throws out his arms and spins.

M. ON CHAPLIN II

In Paris, Marcel Marceau met Charlie Chaplin. Marceau recognized the aging film star at the Orly airport. It was 1967, more than fifty years after the first Little Tramp film and thirty years after the last. Four decades after the talkies dented Chaplin's career for good. Two after the actor was accused of un-American activities. Two after J. Edgar Hoover asked the FBI to keep extensive secret files on him. Fifteen years after he left the US for what he thought would be a brief trip. He was not allowed back in.

In 1967, Chaplin was nearly eighty. His fame was diminished, as was his health. No one else recognized him. Marceau's career was strong. The young mime was making television appearances and signing book deals. He approached Chaplin, and after talk of the weather, Marceau began to imitate the Little Tramp. Then Chaplin imitated Marceau's Little Tramp. Marceau brought his knees to the ground, took the Tramp's hand in his own, and kissed it. He looked up to see Chaplin's cheeks wet with tears.

COLLECTIONS: READING FOR A WELL-ROUNDED EDUCATION

Discourse on Universal History.
(Jacques-Bénigne Bossuet)

Lucan's "Pharsalia."
(Georges de Brébeuf)

White Magic Revealed.
(Henri Decremps)

An Enquiry into the Nature and Place of Hell.
(Tobias Swinden)

Essays.
(Michel de Montaigne)

The Life of Monsieur de Molière.
(Jean Léonor Le Gallois de Grimarest)

The Life of Napoléon.
(Napoléon)

Interesting Letters of Pope Clement XIV.
(Pope Clement XIV)

Elementary Encyclopedia: or, Basics of the Sciences and of the Arts.
(Isaac-Matthieu Crommelin)

On Benefits.
(Seneca)

Provincial Letters.
(Pascal)

The History of the Conspiracy of the Spaniards against the Republic of Venice.
(CésarVichard, M. l'abbé de Saint-Réal)

SCENE 8

A scarf is tied around his face. He tucks a found wallet into his back pocket. A stranger approaches, and the two begin to tango. (Marceau's characters are constantly breaking into dance with women they've only just met.) One of his hands, representing the woman, works its way around his back to feel around for the wallet. The other hand wrestles it back. It's a secondary battle between expressive, sinewy fingers. Fast-forward and the "Paris tough" shows that he's managed to hold on to the wallet.

SCENE 9

He bears an uncanny resemblance to the Count from *Sesame Street*. Perhaps it's the prominent nose and high collar. His velvet cape is deep maroon, lined with tassels. In these scenes, there's no audience, no sound, as if someone forgot to turn on the microphone. The camera zooms in so closely that we can see pink, fleshy tear duct and the veins in his eyes. His irises are light brown. His eyeliner is smudged. There's a little glimpse of the striped sailor shirt peeking out from underneath his cape. He holds up the title card: *Sloth*.

The footage dissolves to Marceau slouched under a blue backdrop and a painted crescent moon. There's no story here. A sleepy guy tries to wake up, but he winds up going back to bed. The dullest of the deadly sins.

Marceau yawns, his body crumpled and weak. He does a few shoulder taps, and then grasps at his lower back in pain. His left leg is crooked, dragging behind him as he walks. He pulls his pants up slowly, fighting with the tangled suspenders, snapping them against his chest, but they fall to his ankles when he takes a step.

He turns on the faucet and splashes water on his face. His arms are too inflexible to reach the back of his neck. He begins the same set of actions as *The Society Party*, painstakingly wrestling with his jacket, gloves, and hat. But then he staggers to the back of the room and sits down. After letting out a heaving yawn, he cracks open a book. His movements get slower as he turns the pages. He goes limp and collapses on the bed, completing the useless circuit of his brief day.

The scene itself is a perfunctory performance, apparently included only to fill a hole in *The Seven Deadly Sins*. There's no story, no interpretation. But *Sloth* opens the door for the more theatrical vices.

SCENE 10

Lust arrives hastily, clocking in at less than two minutes. The beige floor and gray backdrop are suggestive of the beach on an overcast day. Marceau is backlit; his figure casts a long shadow as he works with one hand open as palette and the other holding a brush. He energetically blends colors and applies paint to the canvas. But something distracts him. His gestures slow down, even as he continues work.

50   He steps back and shapes an hourglass figure with his hands—a woman's body. As if this is the first time he's seen his own model. He begins to paint performatively in big, broad strokes—showing off for her. Deciding the brush is too limiting, he throws down his tools and smears paint around the canvas with his hands.

His eyebrows dance up and down suggestively. For a brief moment, he closes his eyes and his mouth pulls back, as if overcome by her beauty. He paints even more vigorously now, but he peers past the canvas for her response. Finally he abandons the canvas and steps forward to kiss her hand.

Time passes. It sputters then stretches. What matters is not the speed of light, but the speed of thought. The mime refashions time, sculpting it with a precision instrument. He can suspend it or hasten it at will. He marches in place for three minutes and a lifetime has passed. In three minutes, eighty-four years.

M. INTERACTS WITH THE PRESS

Now here's some footage of Marceau that's truly silent. No music, no sound effects, no ballet flats striking the stage floor.

In grainy black-and-white film shot in June of 1958, passengers disembark at the Orly airport. A man runs up the stairs, pushing against the crowd to present Marceau with a huge bouquet of flowers. Greetings and kisses hold up the other passengers.

A group of photographers are waiting on the runway. Marceau arrives dressed in a smart three-piece suit, clearly delighted with the welcoming committee. An unidentified blonde woman is there, speaking to Marceau excitedly. He responds to her by pantomiming a man on a motor scooter driving in circles. The camera returns to her wide smile and crooked teeth. Now he mimes holding an umbrella, crouched over and wincing at the rain. The camera pans back again as she tries to hide her impatience. Marceau's pretending to be a pool shark, making a trick shot behind his back. After the successful play, he swallows a huge gulp from a glass. He waves to indicate that he's done with these stunts. He's ready to go. The camera leaves him, focusing instead on the airfield, planes parked in the distance.

Her wait is over. She gets him next.

M. ON MASTERING ONE'S FEELINGS

Marceau was an advocate for fencing and had his students enroll in classes. "Fencing is a school of humility and develops speed, perfect control of the body, balance, beauty, and strong grace. It should be recommended to all men wanting to master their feelings and actions during a lifetime."

Bip pulls the sword out slowly and, looking briefly at the sky, makes the sign of the cross. A woman's hand appears before him, which he of course bends down to kiss. He pulls the delicate fingers towards his lips, only to find her forcing his arms behind his back. Bip is cuffed and led away.

COLLECTIONS: ITEMS FROM JAPAN

This is a little weird, but Marceau had a traditional kendo uniform made—kendo meaning "the way of the sword" in Japanese.

It has wide-legged pants (*hakama*) that resemble a skirt. The protective armor (*bogu*) includes a mask (*men*) with a metal grid covering the face, head, shoulders, and throat; gloves (*kote*) protecting his wrists and forearm; a breastplate (*do*) shielding the belly, ribs, and chest; and the *tare* covering the lower abdomen and upper thighs. The costume is complete with weaponry: one wooden sword (*katana*) and three bamboo swords (*shinai*).

It also came with a jacket (*keikogi*) with "M. Marceau" embroidered on the breast.

COLLECTIONS: KNIVES

There were two from Japan called *wakizashi*. These were the best weapons for seppuku. They looked like miniature katana swords. One of them had a cracked handle, the other a crack in the sheath.

And there was a dagger from the early Bronze Age, Persia. A colorfully rotted blade: green and yellow and brown.

The rest looked like they were bought at a costume shop for an *Arabian Nights*–themed party:

> From Morocco, two knives with round blades and wooden handles.
> Another curvy dagger, this one from the Ottoman Empire, called a *jambiya*.
> A wavy sword from Indonesia called a *keris*. The handle in the shape of a lion, small animals running down the sheath.

COLLECTIONS: MISCELLANEOUS

He was married and divorced three times:
Huguette Mallet, two sons, Michel and Baptiste.
Ella Jaroszewicz, no children.
Anne Sicco, two daughters, Camille and Aurélia.

He bought a farmhouse in Berchéres, an hour outside Paris. There were four trees on the property at the time of purchase. "I have planted more than 2,500 and created a forest."

COLLECTIONS: ICONS

On his walls, saints and angels dressed in red.
Golden orbs around their heads.

Saint George on horseback slaying a dragon. In
the background, you can see a princess locked in
a tower.

Saint John the Evangelist sitting on a chair as he
writes the gospel. John holds a book in his left
hand, a pen in his right, as an eagle cowers at his
feet.

The Ascension of Elijah.

The Archangel Michael and the Archangel Gabriel.
Judgment and Mercy—in movies they are played by
John Travolta and Tilda Swinton. Michael's very
name is a war cry to the angels. He's a prince who
guards Eve's body. They are healers, warriors,
messengers, protectors. They stand side by side in
Notre Dame and side by side in Marceau's home
in Berchéres.

Saint Catherine wears a pretty tiara while seated
on her throne. She holds in her hands the very

breaking wheel to which her own body was once strapped. No kidding, they call it the Catherine wheel now.

Archangel Raphael on a pink background with a fish he would later name Tobias.

Gabriel again, this time holding flowers and a sword. Avoiding his soldier friend.

The warrior Saint Demetrius. He's trampling on a fallen soldier with his horse.

In his house, he hung a life-size painting of Bip, dressed in white—the usual bell-bottoms and sailor's pullover. His arms are stretched out and his feet are together like the crucified Christ. Variants of his own disembodied face float around him: Bip, Bip, Bip, Bip.

There is a photograph of Marceau sitting on an overstuffed couch beneath this painting of Bip. He reclines deep into the seat. His legs are crossed. He looks into the camera, unsmiling.

PIERRE VERRY

A word here on the man who worked as the Presenter of Cards from 1952 to 1979. He accompanied Marceau on nearly six thousand performances, through seventy-five countries.

Marceau was a particular man. The card must be held completely straight, while Verry's arm dangled at an awkward angle, as if halted midstep.

John Beaufort wrote that Verry made "title-card-holding itself a fine art." Frances Herridge marveled at his "immobility that rivals a statue's."

Verry also studied with Decroux. The teacher was obsessed with divorcing mime from narrative, and so he created *le mime statuaire*. "My passion, my zeal for mime . . . grew out of my fervor for sculpture and its sensual, carnal pleasure, which inspired me even as a child." Decroux wanted to imbue theater with these properties.

To Marceau, mime was a kind of riddle. The audience was challenged to recognize the action, identify the character, situate the scene within a story. How to fill the blank spaces?

The lights came up and Verry stood as if petri-fied, holding a black board with white lettering: *The Cage*. The first clue. A starting point for the rest of the performance.

Marceau compared Verry's costume to the etchings of Honoré Daumier and Jacques Callot. Bright yellow and blue feathers stuck out of his oversized hat. Long tassels dangled from his sleeves. He wore rich turquoise leggings. He definitely wasn't Bip.

Clive Barnes wrote of Verry, "He holds, caught up in some frozen moment of heroic poetry, the card announcing Marceau's next miracle. He is quite a minor miracle himself."

The lights faded to black over Verry, and when they rose again, there was Marceau.

But remember. Time is material. You can feel it erode your skin, like wind and rain.

The mime keeps count in heartbeats and breaths.

After decades, he is weathered.

M. ON FAILURE

Anne Sicco was a nineteen-year-old fan who wandered into Marcel Marceau's dressing room. He was approaching fifty. Camille was born. They married. Aurélia was born.

Marceau said, "Does not pantomime offer the language of the heart?"

In old photographs, Anne was slender in a tiered, white dress. Her blonde hair was tied back in a long braid.

In time, she came to teach experimental theater at Marceau's mime school. For years, they kept residence in Paris. In the evenings he read, listened to music, and painted, speaking little to Anne.

She said, "It's a silent sort of exchange."

Perhaps the only one who understood.

"He has silent cries."

She's smiling from behind a camera. Her lens pointed at the leathery face of an old man.

Anne shared her name with his mother.

They divorced in 1984.
She stopped teaching at the school in 1985.
She founded her own company in 1986.

What was all that energy spent on? Women are not worth striving for. The reward is too fleeting, and then the reward is too much.

He said, "My personal life has been very difficult. I have been married three times. The marriages all failed. It's hard to be a family man in my position. When you're traveling all over the world you can't have your wife waiting for you, like Penelope. Now one of my ex-wives is teaching in my school in Paris. We have become very good friends. In this sense, my life is not a failure."

In interviews, he referred to her as his "former wife." Why then did some obituary notices print "survived by his wife Anne Sicco Marceau"?

Aurélia was about to go onstage when she heard that her father had died. Anne was the director. She canceled the performance.

Anne said, "Je ressens une immense douleur."

She said, "C'était un homme qui me fascinait."

"Nous sommes tous bouleversés."

M. ON TECHNOLOGY

In 1974, Marcel Marceau did an ad for Xerox's new color copier. The commercial runs for ninety seconds. Marceau mimics a robot. He pantomimes copying both sides of a sheet of paper and pushing the computer around the office. The ad ends with a guarantee. He says, "Call Marcel Marceau. If no one answers, it's me."

BIP AS SLEEK CREATURE OF THE DEEP

He pushes against the floor to make it look as if he is pushing against a heaviness in the air. The fabric stretches over his torso, clinging to juts of bone, so that a hollow reveals itself. This body is composed of vacancies and devotions. The clothes don't constrict. They wrap around his sinewy limbs like skin. They fit better than his own loose skin. His costume is smooth like a porpoise. The attached red rose is a dorsal fin.

SCENE 11

Marceau clothed in black against a black backdrop. The picture of poverty. His body is crooked and stiff. His eyes stare into the distance, unfocused. It takes a moment to register that he's blind. He's blind. *Alms for the poor*. He holds his hand out. It dips a little each time a passerby presses a coin into his palm. And once his hand is full, he deposits the change into his shirt pocket. He walks off, tapping his way with a cane. His hands brush along the side of a wall until he finds the door handle. He pulls out a key and lets himself in.

He's entered a room filled with gold. He deposits his panhandled coins and gestures upward at stacks of money in front of him. He tries on necklaces, attentive to their delicate clasps. He piles chains around his neck and rings onto his fingers. He lights a cigar and takes a few pleasurable puffs. In this vault of riches, his eyes work just fine.

COLLECTIONS: MASKS

The imported ones came from former French colonies in Africa. Wooden masks from the Bambara tribe of Mali, the Baule and Yaouré tribes of Côte d'Ivoire. They were heavy, dark wood, hybrids of man and animal.

But the Japanese theater masks were the most beloved. He hung them vertically, like a totem pole, down one side of his bookshelf. His daughter later said that he drew from these masks to create Bip's expressive traits.

One is a woman. She's an ideal beauty of the Heian era, with shaved eyebrows, red lips, and blackened teeth.

There's an old-timer smiling. His hair has receded to the crown. He grows a long beard and deep wrinkles crisscross his forehead. His cheekbones cast shadows over his thin face.

There are two demon masks. One, an *oni*, made of ivory. She's a woman, mouth open, eyes golden.

Another frowning face.

Some granddaddies. Their grins surrounded with
trimmed mustaches and goatees.

COLLECTIONS: ZOOMORPH

Two silver roosters, suspended in combat. Combs erect and tail feathers fanned out. Light shines off of their open beaks, their claws, the barbs of their feathers.

A bronze lion bares its long teeth. Chinks of metal broken off its mane. Its face has turned bright green since it was first cast in third-century Rome.

Three ivory elephants, one with a man riding on his back, carved from the very tusks for which they were killed. From China and India, nineteenth-century.

An ambiguous bestial face. Vulpine head ablaze with deranged eyes. An open, drooling mouth connects only at the canines. From the Tumaco-La Tolita culture, sculptors of so many afflicted figurines.

The falcon in Ernest Meissonier's *The Falconer* is a burst of white brushstrokes (the underside of his wings and his compact body), a smear of brown and red (his camouflaged plumage), and some bright yellow streaks (talons). He's a blur of motion, in contrast to the stationary falconer posing to show off his gold-trimmed robe.

A hunting dog gazes affectionately at Général Maisonneuve. The hound is tiny at the commander's boots, all spots and floppy ears.

A white carousel horse coated with polychrome resin stands one and a half meters tall, rearing up on his hind legs. Alarm in his yellow eyes as he strains against his bit.

M. ON VIDEO

He doesn't translate well. His movements are slow.
Disjointed. A bag of bones. Can't hold your atten-
tion. You fast-forward through entire scenes. Did
you go too far? Rewind. Sit through it again. He
seems arrogant. And the silence is interrupted by
a laugh track.

You can clearly see the pancake makeup, the fake
eyebrows, his constant mugging. A stark reminder
of what you've always suspected: he's just a clown.

73

SCENE 12

He is buoyant. The stage floor, a tightrope, a milli-
meter wide. It bends and springs.

No. Not so. Walking against the wind, *pretending* to
walk against the wind, he is less effective than you.
You, on your way to work, proud as you plant your
feet on the ground, step by step.

How is the breeze over there?
Fifty-seven miles per hour. Pedestrians
dodging branches.
Look at that one, tossed here and there.

He'd do and undo each gesture, as if forever tying
and untying a shoelace.

CAMILLE ON MARCEAU

Her father was entirely inhabited by his art. Mime was his way of building a world as he wanted it to be.

She also believed that the house in Berchéres was a physical manifestation of that world. She called his house *a world apart*. She called it *a virtual museum*.

She described strangely lit rooms, colorful tiled windows. She used the words *a place of peace, a childhood dream*. Camille asked us to imagine her as a young girl, coming upon wind-up toys, medieval automatons. She asked us to imagine waiting for her father to come home from tour—sometimes three hundred shows a year. He'd spend hours elaborating on the souvenirs he brought home, piece by piece.

She said it was a home where objects from all cultures coexisted—a setting that could only be staged by an artist. The house filled with objects created another silent space.

COLLECTIONS: ANCIENT DOLLS

Twenty-three figurines:

From the Tumaco–La Tolita culture, the pres-
ent-day border of Ecuador and Colombia (700
BC to 350 AD), they were found beheaded on
garbage dumps, on burial mounds, near the
coastline, as if broken in ritual. Immortalized
in sex, motherhood, illness, and old age. Some
suffered from visible afflictions: Down syn-
drome, dwarfism, facial paralysis, and tumors.
The natives disappeared before the arrival of
the Spanish, but their dolls remained. The sha-
man, the mother, the boy, the warrior.

Four terra cotta statuettes:

Archaic period (3500 to 2000 BC) in what's
now Mexico, right at the development of pot-
tery, the first sign of settling down and accu-
mulating objects. The puny legs, monstrous
heads, and slits for eyes.

More:

Nearly all artifacts of Colima Culture (100
BC to 250 AD) were buried in shaft tombs,

which were then discovered by looters. Dating and provenance are problems. Seated man, coated in a warm orange-brown slip; little guy with round irises and a bob hairdo, his body compact like an urn.

Idol:

The Chancay (1100 to 1400 AD) culture developed along the central coast of Peru. Their ceramic dolls were usually women, almost exclusively black and white, rough to the touch. *Cuchimilco* figure, a symbol of fertility with her engorged belly, her dark nipples, and her short, useless arms.

Vase:

Chimú ceramics, rubbed against rocks until they shined, were made for domestic use and funeral offerings. The Chimú (700 to 1400 AD) worshipped the moon, to which they sacrificed their children, animals, and birds. Terra cotta man with tiny head and round belly, resembling a hen.

COLLECTIONS: PAINTINGS

Mostly seventeenth- and eighteenth-century. Oil on canvas, oak board, copper. One marked with blood. Mostly European. *École Français*, *École Flamande*, *École Genoise*. Some of the brushwork was fine and some was sloppy.

There's *Susanna and the Elders*, an apocryphal story from the Book of Daniel. Look at young Susanna stepping out of the bath in her husband's backyard, wearing only a necklace.

Here's an imagined erotic scene from the violent Greek myth, *Diana and Actaeon*. The nude Diana wraps her arms around Actaeon's thigh. She whispers a curse into his ear, and he leans back to listen.

A strange painting called *The Costume Ball*. The party-goers hold hands. Men and women, their smiling faces illuminated by warm light. They dance in circles. They gossip in twos and threes. Actually, no one is in costume at all except the clown Harlequin, alone and slouching in the foreground.

M. VERSUS M.

Marceau plays seventeen characters. The film is all Marceau. Multiples of Marceau. Ghosts of Marceau. Marceau talking to Marceau. Marceau stealing from Marceau. Marceau dreaming of Marceau. Marceau captaining Marceau. This is star power. This is color.

He is a swimmer who dips his feet into an empty pool. Slowly he lowers his body. Standing firmly on two legs, he imitates the freestyle. The camera shoots him from beneath, so that he's all wrinkles and nostrils. An old man.

He wanders through an empty ship. He has an elaborate set stripped of props. As the captain who stands in an engine room crowded with navigational tools, Marceau mimes a telescope. As a crew member who cleans the ship's wooden deck, Marceau mimes the mop. As the bartender who stands at a stocked bar, Marceau mimes the wine bottle. He's a passenger sitting at a table crowded with fine china, but without food or silverware.

Marceau plays dress-up: Starts off as a stowaway, chest hair poking out of his ragged shirt. Now a gentleman in a tux. Then he appears as a captain in uniform. He comes to you in drag as an old lady. She wears a hat overflowing with fruit.

The camera lens is unforgiving, abrupt. His gestures are cut off. The characters stare at one another. The camera follows their gazes. Marceaus watch other Marceaus, their eyes gleaming with suspicion.

Find a pink handkerchief. Pick it up. Find the girl who lost her handkerchief. Pick her up.

The handkerchief belongs to a young woman. She is dressed head-to-toe in pink. All the Marceaus take notice. They vie for her.

Terry Goldman was a twenty-two-year-old drama student at Moorhead State College in Minnesota. Her only previous role was in the chorus of a school musical. Marceau noticed her working backstage when he performed at Moorhead, and he asked her to appear in his film.

The girl heads back to her room on the ocean liner. Marceau, our captain, follows. She opens the door with a skeleton key. When he rounds the corner, the only trace left of her is a pink handkerchief on the floor. Captain Marceau picks it up delicately.

Another Marceau, this time the well-dressed gentleman, sees her in the ballroom. He lays his hand around her waist and they dance. She is pretty and glassy-eyed as he leans in to kiss her.

COLLECTIONS: JAPANESE DOLLS

Two geriatrics
Two empresses
One princess
Two archers
One old man holding a bow and arrows
Five samurai
One actor dressed as a samurai
One actor and one actress, both wearing Noh masks

SCENE 13

A sign is propped up stage left of the devil: *Pride*.

Marceau wears a newspaper folded in the shape of Napoléon's bicorn hat. He assumes a wide stance, legs straddled apart. He twists a mustache around his finger and takes a minute to admire the medals that decorate his jacket. He paces the stage, walking in stiff, controlled strides, each step punctuated with an audible stomp.

The dusty pink backdrop is streaked with purple and orange, like a striking sunset. The stage floor is pale yellow.

As he walks, the general leads slightly with his head, approaching a chessboard to make a move. He stares rather patronizingly at his opponent and gestures with his hand, *Well, you go ahead*. An air of ease and leisure. Looking down at the board, he chuckles to himself.

Then his opponent's maneuver makes him flinch. Double take, thumps his chest in frustration. With each successive move he shows more strain. His hand stutters, unsure where to land. He side-eyes his opponent. Puts on a monocle to scrutinize the board. Tugs at his collar. Grimaces. His opponent makes another move, and he waves his hands as if to say, *No, I'm out.* He's above this, turns to go, then paces back. Again his heavy footfalls reverberate. He scans the board, as if hoping to make a strategic play, but instead flips the table. Stands there defiantly, pointing to the distance, daring his opponent to walk away. Happily he watches the man's exit, relieved to be alone.

AN INTERVIEW

I'm not sorry.
You should be sorry.
I'm not sorry.

Two hundred shows a year

"Family is not important to me. I have no time
to be a family father. If I had, I would have stayed
in the same town. I would not have toured the
world."

Being there is enough.
I was there.
Where?
Elsewhere.

Three hundred shows a year

Better than dead.
Not so.
Better.

"Marcel Marceau has no private life," said his brother, Alain Mangel, who served as his manager. The reporter Aljean Harmetz described Alain as *expansive* and *chunky*: "His kinship is—if not exactly hidden—definitely not publicized."

SCENE 14

Second movement of Mozart's Piano Concerto
no. 21. Marceau begins with limbs folded. He's
on his knees, fists knotted in front of his face. As
he rises, we can see that his feet are turned out
balletically. Interlaced fingers release from their
tight snarl, and arms undulate like ocean waves.
He transforms from water to fish, bringing his
hands together, thumbs like tiny flippers.

"A body rendered obedient," said Decroux. He
taught his students to isolate each unit of the body.
"The image of the ideal actor" was a marionette.
Marceau learned to unfasten his head from neck,
neck from collarbone, collarbone from rib cage.
Now each finger moves independently. *If I do the
fish, I become the fish, I breathe the water.*

Next, one hand portrays earth. Another, a shoot
springing from the soil. Marceau holds his arms
out as branches. The Tree of Life appears before
us, populated by birds and insects. He folds inward
then rises, this time as Adam, pieced together out
of dust. Man takes his first steps, looks around.
In sleep, he clutches his rib, and out springs Eve.
Again, Marceau gestures the hourglass figure.

Behold her womanly beauty! Adam and Eve walk in place, holding hands. His left hand writhes in the shape of a serpent; the reptile's dirty mouth whispering temptations into Eve's ear. She gazes upon the snake with intrigue and clutches the forbidden fruit. Eve falls backwards—the mime performing a deep backbend, crown of his head grazing the floor. Cowering on the ground, Adam and Eve hold each other—though we see only one. They face an angry God and take their first steps out of Eden.

A TWENTY MINUTE SILENCE FOLLOWED BY APPLAUSE

Sound travels like water, flows into our bodies through inlets and ears. You don't have earlids, after all. We take it in. Flesh absorbs vibrations. Noise beats at your bowels. It taps softly at the roots of tiny hairs that cover your skin. It can tickle or nauseate. The force is invisible, a ghost. Sound agitates your nerves, wind blowing against stalks of grain.

As we watch the mime's expressive form, we lose awareness of our own. We forget to breathe. Thank God our lungs inflate and deflate on their own.

This is why—at performance end—we scream, stomp our feet, and throw our hands together. And we violently reawaken to our bodies.

OTHER WORKS

In Marceau's painting, a mass of faces gaze directly ahead. Hundreds if not thousands of little specks representing people in the far distance. An audience, if you will. Their eyes all focused. Many have stage makeup applied—painted cheeks, dark lipstick. A few are Pierrots, a few nude women with big, round nipples. Their faces are placid, cast in a pink glow.

Another is tinted blue. Again, the mass of faces, eyes forward. Each mouth forms a wide, toothy grin. It's sinister. There are no Pierrots this time, but many in the audience directly resemble Marceau with his wiry hair, deep-set eyes, big nose. Again, the big-chested women in front, barely contained by their bras.

Bip at the Circus. *Bip in the Crowd*. *Bip in the Country*. In *Bip's Dream*, he flies over the tiny city in a dark blue night. In *Bip's Arrest*, a cop apprehends him in front of a crowd of people, in a glowing red city. *The Death of Pierrot and the Birth of Bip*. *Bip Is Possessed by His Dreams*. *Vultures Scrutinize Bip*. *Bip's Imitators*. *The Angel Bip Rises*. Two paintings called *Bip's Despair*.

CLIVE BARNES ON MATERIALISM

"How we love the invisible mantel shelves he so casually leans against."

SCENE 15

All the clichés, the jokes, mimes trapped in invisible boxes come down to this: a man walks along and hits an invisible wall. He jumps back. He can't see the wall, but he can feel it.

He reaches as high as he can and recognizes that the wall extends far above him. He puts one hand forward, then the other, then takes a step. Two hands forward, another step. His eyes light up only as he learns to navigate—feeling around corners, turning ninety degrees, looking for an exit. His mood turns from confounded to desperate. He pounds the surface of the wall with his fist.

The man finds an opening and tries to pry it open. He sticks his head in and looks from side to side. Climbs, shoulders first, and begins walking again. Almost immediately, he smacks into a second wall, stunned by the impact. Again he searches the perimeter, rounding the corners of this secondary space.

As he goes deeper, the room shrinks, evidenced by the actor's increasingly constricted movements. The man is shrinking as well. Finally he dies, body folded into a knot.

Seeing is a way of possessing. With our eyes, we have what we desire. We are in control.

But when we watch the mime, desire turns to envy. Our limbs are incapable of such articulation. Our muscles cannot call upon so deep a vocabulary.

We're jealous of the volume and range of his movements. We cannot even mimic the gestures. Bip's passions are not for us.

93

M. WRITES ABOUT M.

Marcel Marceau signed a deal in 1965 to write an autobiography. He titled it *My Silent Cry*. It was slated for release in 1970.

In 1983, he said in an interview, "Now they are desperate. But I don't think the book is late. It's ripe to come out now. I feel I'm in my prime. If I had died during the sixties I would not have been 'achieved.' I know time is running out. I have now ten years of full power. If I'm not better now than I was ten years ago I would have stopped. How could I tell? The public."

By 2007, the year he died, the memoir was still not published. And the world never knew what Marcel Marceau wept for, openly or privately, silently or aloud.

BIP THE STOIC

He doesn't exactly "take it like a man." Too sensitive for that. When the butterfly's wings stop beating, when it wilts in his fingers, when it devolves to more insect and less flower, the corners of Bip's lips tilt. His eyes hollow out. He turns into a mannequin. But he doesn't cry.

Bip's predecessor Pedrolino was the baby of the mime family. He bawled when his wife Franceschina was unfaithful, guilt-ridden over crimes he did not commit. He sobbed when he was caught and punished for playing tricks on Pantaloon and the Doctor, tricks he himself was tricked into playing. He lamented when he was beaten by his masters. He blubbered when he was given a plate of spaghetti, tears streaming down his face with each bite.

SCENE 16

He is not exactly a comedian. Not a tragedian. He swings between these two poles. His face is a metronome, his mouth its needle.

COLLECTIONS: CLOCKS

He had seventeen:

Nine of them were gold.

One had a blue enamel sky and cherubs circling
the dial.

Another was engraved with butterflies.

One was actually a sundial.

One was a train conductor's watch.

The watches were mostly from the 1800s, but one
was from the reign of Napoléon III and
another from the reign of Louis XVI.

They were signed by the watchmakers: Gille Bois-
dechesne, Vacheron Constantin, Courtecui-
sse, Johan Schrettegger in Augsburg, Joslin
and Park.

The Breguet was a fake. (Did Marceau know?)

You are ever the beholder, the authority, the eye.

He is always performer, the perceived, a puppet doomed to traffic in symbols, a constant stream of new gestures to calcify cliché. He is the life-sized marionette, tumbling for our amusement.

His fingers tickle at your ribs. You shudder and sigh. You are a bag of hot air, squeezed in his grip. Maybe he was in charge all along.

What happens then?

You call him genius, master, icon, greatest.

And he agrees: "I know what I am worth. If Marcel Marceau did not know what he was worth, he would be in trouble."

M. ON MOST MIMES

On Marcel Marceau's second tour of America, he returned to find mimes trapped in imaginary boxes on every street corner. Mimes at Thirty-Fourth and Eighth. Mimes at Forty-Sixth and Seventh. Mimes in Central Park. Mimes at Lincoln Center.

A journalist asked Marcel Marceau what he thought of the copycats.

Marceau responded, "It's better than mugging people."

A journalist asked Marcel Marceau why most Americans hate mime.

Marceau responded, "Because most mimes are lousy."

Marcel Marceau said, "A great artist in mime has pupils with whom he works regularly, often throughout his whole life, and who in turn carry on the traditions they have learned from their master. But sometimes, when the mime gets old and dies, and his pupils have become very few, the art fades into obscurity. We have to wait for a great new artist to arrive to carry on the tradition and add his own work of advancement."

He lobbied the French government for ten years to build a mime school. Thirteen times, he asked for an audience with President Valéry Giscard d'Estaing.

"Either France will give me a subsidy or I will go to America. France owes this to me."

Two American universities offered to fund the mime school. In 1978, France gave him two hundred thousand dollars.

He said, "If it had been done in America, it would have been two million. I would have said yes, but I am a masochist."

The Marcel Marceau International School of Mimodrama no longer exists. The building still stands on rue René Boulanger. A dance studio.

Marcel Marceau said, "I knew I would die one day. I didn't want people to say, 'Oh, he was the only mime in existence.'"

COLLECTIONS: PERFORMING DOLLS

A set of shadow puppets from 1890.

Two mechanical dolls also from the late nineteenth century. The woman is dressed like a trickster, the man like a Renaissance-era patrician. They were meant to be mounted onto a street organ, striking their carillon bells in time. But for now they stand unanchored. The man's instrument is missing, so his hand is suspended holding air.

Wind-up Turkish magician from the French manu-
facturer La Maison Rambour, circa 1898. Baby face, glassy blue eyes, and an open mouth. He's porcelain, dressed in a turban. When you crank him up, he lifts a silk pouch to reveal a snake hiding underneath. He sticks out his tongue in surprise and waves his wand to wish the serpent away.

COLLECTIONS: SACRED DOLLS

Eighteenth-century Burma: statuette of a monk holding his hands in anjali mudra position.

Eighteenth-century Cambodia: bronze torso of Vishvakarman, the creator, meditating in dhyana mudra position.

Twentieth-century Tibet: the wrathful god Mahakala with three heads and six arms, one broken hand.

Nineteenth- and twentieth-century China:
Buddha gilded in lacquered wood, sitting between two Guanyin Bodhisattva.
A divinity seated on a lion's back.
Three Gods of War.

European gods and saints, carved from wood, seventeenth- and eighteenth-century:

God the Father, crowned and sitting on a throne. The hem of his red robe grazes the floor. A disheveled old man, loose gray hair held in place by a heavy crown. Shards are chipped off from his high forehead and narrow nose.

Saint George on horseback, towering over a tiny, doomed dragon.

Saint Martin sharing his cloak with a beggar, his saber still drawn.

Saint Anne instructing the Virgin. The paint has worn off both women, and the Virgin's head is missing. Anne's voluminous cloak is suspended in motion, as if tossed by an incessant wind.

Two baby Jesuses manufactured in different countries. The Italian Lord and Savior has a fat belly, his infant dick dangling. He's at play, distracted by some wonder of nature. The Spaniard is pious, thin, and swaddled in a baggy diaper. He looks forward, provocation in his eyes.

"I do not practice religion but when I do 'Creation of the World,' God enters in me."

Three diverse kings ride out to greet the Lord. One bearded, another boyish, and the last is an African king. His hands are brown, but his face is painted jet black, vividly setting off his gold crown.

M. ON THE KING OF POP

Marcel Marceau had sympathy for Michael Jackson. He saw in Michael Jackson something of himself.

"Michael has the soul of a mime," he said.

What is this soul of a mime? What is shared by Marceau and Michael and all actors who stand onstage making various gestures?

"The soul of a mime is a complex one: part child and part artist, part clown and part tragic figure."

"I've seen Michael on TV for years, and I think that he is a poet. But now he is in the tradition of French poets like Verlaine and Rimbaud because his subject is the lost childhood."

On December 4, 1995, Michael Jackson promoted an HBO special at the Beacon Theater. His career was at its pinnacle.

More than a decade earlier, Jackson modeled the moonwalk after Marceau's *Walking Against the Wind*. And ever since, he had been turning his focus, ever so slowly, away from the voice and toward the body. In a few days, he would collapse from exhaustion. But that night he faced the reporters.

One yelled, "Are you still married?"

Another, "Say hello!"

All questions received the same response: silence.

Instead, Jackson brought out a mime to speak for him.

"For the first time, the King of Mime will work with the King of Pop."

Two men on stage with pancaked faces and liquid bodies. Held under a beam of bright light, Michael Jackson performed the invisible box routine. A metaphor for both their lives.

The journalist Neil Strauss agreed that Michael Jackson was evolving. He wrote: "After Mr. Jackson's collapse, a medical technician said there was so much makeup on his face that medics had to lift his shirt to check his complexion."

It was the winter of 1944–45, harsh, inclement and without heat. Marceau at the time was known only as the most brilliant of Decroux's students. The spectacle of these two men solemnly at work, dripping with sweat in the frigid air, had something admirably crazy about it which spiced their work. The teacher was serious to the point of being comic; he demonstrated an impeccable technique, but was strained in the search for the original and the creative. But the budding mime burst forth with originality, with facility, spirit and charm which are the signs of the artist.

—Marc Beigbeder, philosopher and journalist

M. ON THERIESENSTADT

"At Theriesenstadt, the concentration camp, the Nazis used to show outside visitors that the camps were humane. The Nazis asked the Jewish prisoners, many of whom were musicians, what they would like to perform for the Red Cross, which was going to visit.

"They said the 'Verdi Requiem.' The Nazis laughed. But when they performed it, the Nazis were so moved they stood and applauded.

107

"It didn't change the fact that two weeks later, all the musicians were exterminated."

(1999)

FROM *MARCEL AND ME: A MEMOIR OF LOVE, LUST, AND ILLUSION*

by Paulette Frankl:

"His dominant French nose gave me pause to fantasize the corresponding length of other body parts."

"I was startled by his short stature and knocked aback by his pungent bad breath."

"The open kimono and low cut of his costume revealed his pleasantly hairy chest."

"From a distance, I thought he was a woman!"

"His flesh was as soft as a jellyfish."

"I was the object of his feeding frenzy."

"I was pleased to discover that not all parts of his body were equally subject to the aging process."

"He was all about control."

"He cherry-picked his women from an abundant pool of the young and beautiful."

"'I'll call you.'"

COLLECTIONS: THE FURNITURE

Hailed from Aquitaine, Venice, Basque Provinces. Dented, scratched, distressed, banged into, worn, restored. Reminiscent of *Beauty and the Beast*, those curvy wooden bodies balanced on tiny feet, about to burst into song. Dating to the Regency period, Restoration era.

Louis XIII—Pair of armchairs, walnut painted dark, twisted along the stretcher and arms. High back, moulded walnut, acanthus leaves cut into the arms. Sheep-bone reproduction with broken feet and upholstered wings.

Louis XIV—Bracket clock with brass inlaid red tortoiseshell.

Louis XV—Silver candelabra, four branches reaching out. Chair made of walnut with a violone back. Triangular cabinet that tucks neatly into a corner, its curved front panel restrained by a natural cherry beaded belt.

Louis XVI—Armoire of walnut wood, grooved and lacquered gray. Armchair balanced on tapered beechwood feet. Trumeau mirror carved and gilded with a gold trophy. Pair of bronze candle vases adorned with laurel wreaths, ribbons, and fluted columns.

Louis Vuitton—Two small briefcases, damaged.

COLLECTIONS: THE BOXES

Forged from silver
Rectangular. Hinged, lined with purple cloth
Square. Hammered flourishes and a wooden core
Round. Engraved with scenes from Japan
Engraved snuffbox. Vermilion fabric inside

Flown in from Asia
Japanese painted wooden box
Bronze vault from India
Tea box from Guangzhou
Four Chinese porcelain miniatures
Elm jewelry box from China, missing a mirror

Other
Twenty-one in Russian lacquer
Safe of moulded oak, sealed shut with a wrought
    iron lock
Oval brass, engraved with a character in a frock coat
Safe with studded leather, brass handle, and
    wrought iron pull rings
Disc-playing music box, glossy black with gold
    frills, bearing the inscription "symphonio
    brevete patante"
Pirate's chest

CRITICS ON AGING

"There is always something rather sad about any performing artist who fails to realise that his career is over, but Marcel Marceau is riding on his name and past achievements to such a degree that one's patience and pity is beginning to run out." (Emma Manning, *Stage and Television Today*, 1998)

Does aging give us wisdom? Does it make us stubborn?

A telegram from the brain: Its signals are lost in a neuron forest. Water floods into the organ's grooves. But the mime continues to perform.

"For me two hours of Marceau is like being trapped in a bar with an accomplished raconteur who insists on telling endless shaggy-dog stories." (Edward Thorpe, *The London Evening Standard*, 1984)

Brain cells bloom. Run wild. A fistful scatter in the wind.

"Every action is grossly overplayed, every facial expression exaggerated and the humor is at least fifty years out of date. The characters cannot even read a newspaper without looking like rabbits chomping grass." (Manning)

SCENE 17: BIP HUNTING BUTTERFLIES

Bip is a child. He joyfully runs from one end of the stage to another with an imaginary net, chasing after a bug.

Bip is an old man hunting butterflies. His exaggerated movements are heavy with sentiment. He tries to capture the butterfly in his hands, but he misses, dismay plain on his face.

The body of an animal is a heat engine. The heart's a force pump, growing bigger and slower as we age.

Cat and mouse is a game with consequences. Finally, Bip catches the butterfly. It dies in his hands as he tries to hold it. He brings it to his ears to listen for a heartbeat.

Marceau came up with the butterfly routine in a movie theater when he was fourteen. At the end of *All Quiet on the Western Front*, a butterfly flutters over the barrel of a soldier's gun. As the young man reaches over the trench to touch the butterfly, he gives away his position to an enemy sniper.

BIP GETS LEFT BEHIND

Bip bobs along the skyline, suspended by a red balloon.

His knuckles are pale.

The string is looped twice around his wrist and tied in a sailor's knot.

His right hand lost sensation hours ago, but he doesn't notice.

He wonders, if he falls, how hard will he hit the ground?

M. ON AGING

"Death intervenes."

The inelegance of it
No comedy nose
Goodbye false eyelashes
Farewell large ears
The corners of his lips turn south

"To be sure, he has a voice like someone's grand-
mother." (Maralyn Lois Polak, columnist)

marcel marceau
pere lachaise   mime   charlie chaplin
buster keaton   auschwitz   coffin

Death is always nearby for mimes who drink a glass
of wine with an empty hand, waltz with no part-
ner, who laugh and cry and not a soul can hear.

The ascetic avoided liquor, tobacco, red meat,
and yet a perforated ulcer at sixty-three in Mos-
cow. Emergency surgery, flew to Paris for a subse-
quent operation.

In a photograph taken at the University of Massachusetts, sorority girls screamed in pleasure. They stood next to a snow sculpture carved for their winter carnival. Marcel Marceau wearing a sheepskin. A luxurious white fluffy hat. A discreet red band signifying France's Legion of Honor on his lapel.

Some critics were convinced he was improving.

Andrew Risik wrote, "He is very good at the preposterous dignity with which people try to redeem their worst accidents."

Marceau: "I'm the Picasso of mime. At eighty, Picasso was young. If I keep my fitness, I have at least another ten years. It's an encouragement for all men in their fifties, sixties, and seventies. I don't think of age. I think of life force and creation."

By 1993, Marceau had racked up some fifteen thousand performances in more than one hundred countries.

On tour, Marceau caught the flu but didn't miss an engagement. He said, "Theater people, if we are not seen, we don't exist, we are nothing."

Mayor Rudy Giuliani proclaimed March 19, 1999, "Marcel Marceau Day." Marceau celebrated his seventy-sixth birthday onstage at the Kaye Playhouse in New York City.

You go on. You go on. And there is no fault to it. A man who is doing what he has always done. Chaplin in film, Marceau in theater.

Fans jump up and shout, "You should never be allowed to die."

The mind goes first, then the body. The lightning storm fades to black. Neurons and synapses lose their charge. Proteins shatter, a pile of shards in a dustpan, loose pebbles in a kaleidoscope. This is the brain as it angles and plaques over.

Marceau died on a Saturday in Paris. Emmanuel Vacca, his former assistant, announced it on France Info radio. But he withheld the cause of death.

When the brain shrinks, the sufferer has trouble with language.

Why worry about a mime who has trouble with language?

PÈRE LACHAISE CEMETERY

Three hundred mourners gathered on a chilly autumn day. Some held roses and carnations, which they threw onto the coffin. Others placed stones beside the gravesite. They weathered the light rain without umbrellas.

Mozart by request. "When I do 'The Creation of the World,' I play the second movement of the Piano Concerto no. 21. I have the impression Mozart wrote it for me," Marceau once said.

From underneath a white tent the Rabbi René-Samuel Sirat led the ceremony: three psalms in Hebrew translated into French. He spoke about Marceau's "silence" and "equanimity." He read the Mourner's Kaddish and reminded the crowd that Marceau died on Yom Kippur.

The coffin was cloaked with the French tricolor. A maroon velvet cushion displayed Marceau's medals from France: the Legion of Honor and the National Order of Merit.

Bip's hat was positioned on a pedestal, the same hat that would fetch 3,201 Euros at auction. But that day it stood between Marceau's relatives and body. A towheaded boy carried purple flowers. A teenager's tear fell to the bottom of her chin.

The mourners gathered in division 21, near the very center of the cemetery where the footing is loose, gray gravel. It took many months for a proper headstone to be installed. His family chose a creamy white marker carved with the Star of David. Until then, the gravesite was covered in artificial grass, a combination of real and artificial flowers, leaves that fell from the towering trees, and a plastic sign that read *Marcel Marceau 1923–2007*.

COLLECTIONS: PLEASURE READING

The Divine Comedy. (Dante Alighieri)

The Devil in Paris. (Gavarni)

The Courtiers Manual Oracle; or, The Art of Prudence. (Baltasar Gracián)

Dombey and Son. (Charles Dickens)

The Year 2440: A Dream If Ever There Was One. (Louis-Sébastien Mercier)

Julie; or, The New Heloise. (Jean-Jacques Rousseau)

Marilou. (Serge Gainsbourg and Alain Bonnefoit)

Canto General. (Pablo Neruda)

100 Love Sonnets. (Pablo Neruda)

Art of Birds. (Pablo Neruda)

Total: 2,970 Euros

COLLECTIONS: SILVERWARE

He owned more than 585 kilograms of silver. A pile of ladles, saltshakers, and candlesticks. Five sets of Peruvian stirrups: small silver shoes with pointy toes, engraved with flowers. He had two sets of spurs, radiating little daggers to poke into horseflesh. An empty gun holster decorated with leaves.

Total: 10,610 Euros

COLLECTIONS: ROMAN TABLEWARE FROM THE SECOND CENTURY

blue and green iridescent goblets
bottle that flares out white and pink
paunchy green jar
shallow cup, ultramarine shine clings on
vial's neck tapers into a sharp cylinder
vase's belly adorned with stripes
oil lamp in bronze patina

Total: 2,700 Euros

AFTER M.

Nine hundred of his belongings were auctioned off: paintings, religious icons, clocks, books, knives, wooden dolls, masks, five sailor suits—in gray, navy, white, cream, and black and white—the battered top hat with a single red rose, and a black chair painted with the words "Bip's dreams."

The auction was held over two sunny summer days at Hôtel Drouot, a large auction house in the 9th arrondissement of Paris, the atmosphere described by one reporter as "bazaar-like." Fans, private collectors, and art merchants huddled together. They flipped through piles of photographs. They left their fingerprints on display cases. They picked over Marceau's correspondence, his silverware, his large collection of curios. Nineteenth-century wind-up fortune-teller doll, anyone?

A twenty-eight-year-old art apprentice who couldn't afford any of the objects furiously recorded the starting and final sale prices of as many of Marceau's possessions as she could. "I guess coming here sort of let me feel like I could get inside *le mime* Marceau's world for the last time before it gets split up," she told a reporter.

The walls were crowded with salon-style picture frames: Marceau's own artwork, the paintings he collected, and paintings depicting him. Photographs with Bill Clinton, Cary Grant, Yul Brynner, Ginger Rogers, Maurice Chevalier, Michael Jackson. Masks were mounted on the walls, including multiple reproductions of his own disembodied face.

A mannequin displayed Marceau's gray and white sailor suit. Bip's top hat rested in a glass case at the center of the room. Up close, the fabric was a pale version of black and the rose just some bunched up red lace, fastened to a piece of wire.

"For those of us who knew Marcel and how he lived his life and art as one, this random dispersal of his possessions is very painful," Marceau's musical director Stephan Martell said. He and Marceau's assistant, Valérie Bochenek, attempted to purchase as many items as they could. They hoped to put together what they called "A Museum for Bip." They fell short of the $135,000 they hoped to raise. Still, during the first day, Bochenek made ten successful bids totaling nearly $7,560.

In fact, no one wanted the auction, which was brought about by court order. Even the auctioneer, Rodolphe Tessier, called the event "unfortunate and exceptionally rare." He priced the items low, to all but guarantee that everything would go.

This was Marceau's family's only way to pay back almost half a million Euros in loans. "We tried everything not to have to resort to this, in vain," his daughter Camille said. She added that her father was "humiliated" by his debts. He once said to her in tears, "I've worked like a horse and I've failed in my life."

M. ON TRUTH

"Who in the twentieth century has been world famous as a soloist in mime?" Marcel Marceau asked the journalist Robert Butler in an interview with *The Independent* in 1995.

"Who?"

"I ask you the question. Who?"

"You?"

"Absolutely. It is the truth. You spoke the truth. What I did as a one-man show throughout the world, no one can do again in the twentieth century. Maybe in the twenty-first. I don't know."

Marceau seemed to dismiss the two hundred students who were currently enrolled in his school and the nine performers in his mime company. He taught them the grammar he used to carry out his illusions. They learned to reproduce his gestures faithfully. And when they succeeded in mirroring the master, they began to unravel the art.

"Marceau's success has inspired imitators far and wide, few worth looking at. Mime's gotten a bum rap. Watching Marcel Marceau has a marvelous restorative effect. He can say more with one eyebrow or one ripple of the fingers than would-be clones can do with their entire bodies," Janice Berman wrote in *Newsday* in 1995.

Mime and *Marceau* have become interchangeable. Audiences have a hard time imagining the art form beyond his white face, barren stage, sailor suit, and above all, silence.

Remember, it was Deburau who turned Pierrot into a mute, at the insistence of French authorities. Napoléon barred speech from playhouses to protect France's official state-run theaters, continuing the tradition of Louis XIV, XV, and XVI. Before Deburau's *pantomime blanche*, Pedrolino's chatty family improvised speech and acrobatics in the commedia. Greek and Roman mime performances were accompanied by song and narration from the chorus. Mime hasn't been silent all that long.

In addition to wordless performances, Marceau and Deburau had one other thing in common. Both men died and appeared to take everything down with them. "The genius of Deburau had been replaced by a long succession of imitators who recreated the outward form, but had lost the inner fire; pantomime was an affair of the hands and face, the body covered by voluminous garments," wrote Thomas Leabhart in 1998.

In 1945, when twenty-two-year-old Marcel Marceau sat down in the darkened cinema and watched *Les Enfants du Paradis*, did he foresee his own ascent?

SCENE 18

A fetus uncurls, like a fern. His back straightens.
Chest inflates. The force of air fills his lungs.
His stride turns graceful and robust. The vigor
of youth progresses easily into the confidence
and control of middle age. But this lasts only a
minute. The actor appears full strength not even
half of his three-minute performance. He slows
down. Limbs tense, steps stir, face grows twisted
and eyes blank. The walk becomes a crawl, body
contracting and vivacity fading from his face. A
moment before the stage light drops, death perfectly resembles birth.

SOURCES

Andriotakis, Pamela. "Silence, Please! France's Genius of Mime, Marcel Marceau, Is Bringing His Art to the U.S. Once Again." *People*, February 12, 1979. http://people.com/archive /silence-please-frances-genius-of-mime -marcel-marceau-is-bringing-his-art-to -the-u-s-once-again-vol-11-no-6/.

Aouli, Rachid. "Marcel Marceau Laid to Rest in Paris." *USA Today*, September 26, 2007. http:// usatoday30.usatoday.com/news/world/2007 -09-26-524348347_x.htm.

Associated Press. "Marcel Marceau Auction Nets Nearly 500,000 Euros." *San Diego Union-Tribune,* May 27, 2009. http://www .sandiegouniontribune.com/sdut-eu-france -marcel-marceau-052709-2009may27-story .html.

BBC. "Marcel Marceau Debt Auction Ends." *BBC News* (online), May 27, 2009. http://news .bbc.co.uk/2/hi/europe/8069362.stm.

Butler, Robert. "La Grande Illusion." *The Independent*, January 7, 1995. http://www

.independent.co.uk/arts-entertainment
/la-grande-illusion-1567088.html.

CBC Arts. "Fans, Colleagues Upset Over Auction
of Mime Marcel Marceau's Personal Effects."
CBC News (online), May 25, 2009. http://www
.cbc.ca/news/entertainment/fans-colleagues
-upset-over-auction-of-mime-marcel
-marceau-s-personal-effects-1.800427.

Clarity, James F., and Eric Pace. "Marcel
Marceau, Renowned Mime, Dies at 84." *New
York Times*, September 24, 2007. http://www
.nytimes.com/2007/09/24/arts/24marceau
.html.

Crumley, Bruce. "Marcel Marceau's Not-So-Silent
Auction." *Time*, May 27, 2009. http://
content.time.com/time/world
/article/0,8599,1901182,00.html.

DeWitt, David. "Marceau, Stuck Inside a Hat,
Says, ''." *New York Times*, October 28, 2000.
http://www.nytimes.com/2000/10/28
/theater/theater-review-marceau
-stuck-inside-a-hat-says.html.

Dorcy, Jean. *The Mime, and Essays by Etienne Decroux,
Jean-Louis Barrault, and Marcel Marceau*. New York:
Speller, 1961.

"Eight London Newspaper Magazine Reviews of a Performance at the Old Vic." Review of Marcel Marceau, Old Vic, London. August 20–September 15, 1984. *London Theatre Record* IV, no. 17 (1984). In the collection of the Billy Rose Theatre Division. New York Public Library for the Performing Arts, New York.

Felner, Mira. *Apostles of Silence: The Modern French Mimes.* Rutherford, NJ: Fairleigh Dickinson University Press, 1985.

Frankl, Paulette. *Marcel & Me: A Memoir of Love, Lust, and Illusion.* Santa Fe, NM: Lightning Rod Publications, 2014.

Garcia, Jean-Luc. "Le mime Marceau s'est éteint à Cahors." *La Depeche,* September 24, 2007. http://www.ladepeche.fr/article /2007/09/24/23109-le-mime-marceau-s -est-eteint-a-cahors.html.

Leabhart, Thomas. *Modern and Post-modern Mime.* New York: St. Martin's Press, 1989.

Lust, Annette. *From the Greek Mimes to Marcel Marceau and Beyond: Mimes, Actors, Pierrots, and Clowns; A Chronicle of the Many Visages of Mime in the Theatre.* Lanham, MD: Scarecrow Press, 2000.

Marceau, Aurélia. "Lectures Spectacles 2015–2016." Theatrical program from L'Oeil du Silence. http://www.crl-midipyrenees.fr/wp-content/uploads/2014/12/Dossier_Presse_Loeil_du_silence.pdf.

Marceau, Marcel. "1950–1987." Clippings. MWEZ + n.c. 18,852. Billy Rose Theatre Division. New York Public Library for the Performing Arts, New York.

Marceau, Marcel. "1955–1965 in the USA." Clippings. MWEZ + n.c. 27,753. Billy Rose Theatre Division. New York Public Library for the Performing Arts, New York.

Martin, Ben. *Marcel Marceau: Master of Mime*. New York: Paddington Press, 1978.

Samuel, Henry. "Marcel Marceau's Black Hat and Red Rose Auctioned in Paris." *The Telegraph*, May 26, 2009. http://www.telegraph.co.uk/news/celebritynews/5390047/Marcel-Marceaus-black-hat-and-red-rose-auctioned-in-Paris.html.

Silence Community. "Le Mime Marceau." YouTube video, 28:43. Excerpt from the French television program *Bienvenue*. First broadcast November 2, 1966. Posted

September 6, 2012. https://www.youtube.com/watch?v=EG8A3r2Rcg8.

Stage. "Eloquence Without Words: The Art of Marcel Marceau." Feb 14, 1952.

T-Clippings: Marceau, Marcel. Billy Rose Theatre Division. New York Public Library for the Performing Arts, New York.

Tessier & Sarrou & Associés. "Le Mime Marceau (1923–2007)." Auction catalog: May 26–27, 2009. Bibliorare.com; 2 pdfs. http://www.bibliorare.com/cat-vent_drouot26-5-09-1.pdf; http://www.bibliorare.com/cat-vent_drouot26-5-09-3.pdf.

Tessier & Sarrou & Associés. "Le Mime Marceau (1923–2007) : La Vie D'un Mythe Francais Aux Encheres Acte I - Lot 1 à 500, Mardi 26 Mai 2009." Auction website. http://www.neret-tessier.com/html/index.jsp?id=4163&lng=fr&npp=10000.

Tessier & Sarrou & Associés. "Le Mime Marceau (1923–2007) : La Vie D'un Mythe Francais Aux Encheres Acte II - Lot 501 à 901, Mercredi 27 Mai 2009." Auction website. http://www.neret-tessier.com/html/index.jsp?id=4165&lng=fr&npp=10000.

ACKNOWLEDGMENTS

Parts of this book appeared in *Seneca Review* and *Iowa Review*. Research was supported by a grant from the Royce Foundation.

I'm grateful to the following mimes who granted me interviews and allowed me to observe per-formances and rehearsals. Their inventiveness and reverence informed much of this work: Ivan Bacciocchi, Gyöngyi Biro, Wolfram von Bodecker, Alexander Neander, Maxime Nourissat, Angélique Petit, Lorin Eric Salm, and Elena Serra.

Tim Chartier and Gemma de Choisy made crucial introductions. Mira Felner's elucidating writing on mime allowed a novice to wade into its history and theory. Insights from Mika De Brito changed the course of this work.

My deepest gratitude to the Sarabande staff: Ariel Lewiton, Kristen Radtke, Emma Aprile, Danika Isdahl, and especially my editors Sarah Gorham and Kristen Miller, who elevated my writing and made this book a book.

All of my thanks to Thalia Field, whose own work broke my definitions of literature. My gratitude also to Beth Taylor, Catherine Imbriglio, Roger Mayer, and Richard Eder. What exceptional luck to come across you all as teachers.

Linda Vaughn first saw the light.

With joy and gratitude to my friends, who saw me through early drafts, and in turn offered advice, warmth, and humor (and beverages and a place to crash): Hannah Begley, Nick Chung, Sean Cole, Alexander Eichler, Alexandra Kleeman, Bourree Lam, Caitlin McKenna, Lauren Moseley, Kara Oehler, Amanda Shapiro, Lauren Spohrer, Ben Stark, Kevin Tang, and Dayna Tortorici.

I'm thankful to my parents, 问銀鸽 and 何惧, for their love and steadfastness.

And, finally, to Klaus: my fiercely intelligent, generous, and handsome man.

SHAWN WEN is a writer, radio producer, and multi-media artist. Her writing has appeared in *n+1*, *The New Inquiry*, *Seneca Review*, *Iowa Review*, *White Review*, and the anthology *City by City: Dispatches from the American Metropolis* (Faber and Faber / n+1, 2015). Her radio work has broadcast on *This American Life*, *Morning Edition*, *All Things Considered*, *Here and Now*, and *Marketplace*, and she is currently a producer at Youth Radio. Her video work has screened at the Museum of Modern Art, the Camden International Film Festival, and the Carpenter Center at Harvard University. She holds a BA from Brown University and is the recipient of numerous fellowships, including the Ford Foundation Professional Journalism Training Fellowship and the Royce Fellowship. Wen was born in Beijing, raised in the suburbs of Atlanta, Georgia, and currently resides in San Francisco.

SARABANDE BOOKS is a nonprofit literary press located in Louisville, KY, and Brooklyn, NY. Founded in 1994 to champion poetry, short fiction, and essay, we are committed to creating lasting editions that honor exceptional writing. For more information, please visit sarabandebooks.org.